Rub·ber Room *(noun)*

A confining mind-set where thoughts and possibilities bounce aimlessly

Praise for Unlocking Your Rubber Room

Fresh, funny, lively, engaging every inch of the way. Perry creates an enormously entertaining book worthy not only for teachers and students, but all readers who love good books.

> ~ Professor Richard Walter — Screenwriting Chair, UCLA Film School, and author of *Screenwriting: The Art, Craft and Business of Film and Television Writing, The Whole Picture: Strategies for Screenwriting Success in the New Hollywood,* and the acclaimed novel, *Escape from Film School.*

Passionate and enthusiastic, just like Perry's live presentations. A great blend of practical and real world tips.

> ~ Sue Savage, PHR, MSHR — Human Resources Professional

Professor Binder writes like he teaches — a combination of wisdom and wit as entertaining as it is constructive.

> ~ Adam Israelov — Candidate on Donald Trump's hit show *The Apprentice,* and Perry's former student

Perry presents an easy to read, laugh out loud, behind the scenes look at the life of a non-traditional college professor. Having known Perry for many years, I know for a fact that his universal lessons are based on his own life story, which makes the book that much more endearing and inspirational.

> ~ Scott Frank – Attorney and author of *Buy Low, Sell High, Rent Smart* and *Buy Even Lower: The Regular People's Guide to Real Estate Riches*

UNLOCKING YOUR RUBBER ROOM

44 Off-the-Wall Lessons to Lighten and Transform EVERYDAY LIFE

by Lawyer-turned-Teacher

PERRY BINDER, J.D.

Langdon Street Press
212 3rd Avenue North, Suite 570
Minneapolis, MN 55401
612.455.2293
www.langdonstreetpress.com

All of the events in this book are true as I remember them, unless otherwise noted. Names of individuals mentioned have been changed if they appear in quotation marks. This book is for educational purposes only and does not contain or offer legal advice.

ISBN - 978-1-934938-24-9
ISBN - 1-934938-24-6
LCCN - 2008942175

Book sales for North America and international:
Itasca Books, 3501 Highway 100 South, Suite 220
Minneapolis, MN 55416
Phone: 952.345.4488 (toll free 1.800.901.3480)
Fax: 952.920.0541; email to orders@itascabooks.com

Cover Design by Jenni Wheeler
Typeset by Tiffany Laschinger

Printed in the United States of America

For Bridget, Kevin, and Emily

For Anthony, "Callie," and every student who walks into my classroom

In memory of Jan Wilcox, a person of compassion and action

Table of Contents

Prologue   13

I – Orientation   15

II – 44 Lessons   21

A. Law & Negotiation: Padding Your Rubber Room   21

1. It's good to be the judge! (Part I)   23
2. Finding leverage is the key to enforcing a contract   27
3. In deal making, make the other side feel like a hero   29
4. Stay home! Don't go to work!!   31
5. Always have a sandwich bag, a cell phone, and a big mouth   33
6. Buying a car from a dealer is like a New York City street fight   35
7. How to get a lawyer to return your call   37
8. Lay low, very low, in the weeds (Part I)   39
9. Getting too lawyered up can leave you with nothing   41
10. Sometimes your mother is all you really need   43
11. Nothing is funny in law   45
12. Just because it's legal, doesn't mean it's moral   47
13. Lay low, very low, in the weeds (Part II)   49
14. Sometimes, life can be murder. Or not.   51
15. Company lawyers think we are really stupid   53

EXAM 1: A car, a coffee, a scream   55

B. Potpourri: Organizing Your Rubber Room   57

16. Sometimes you need to suck it up and wing it   59

17. Know the consequences of no regrets   61

18. Figure out if you are a "structure" person or someone who can self-motivate at any given time   63

19. Your computer's "spell check" is not the same as proofreading   65

20. Why not us?   67

21. Sometimes we all need a Cyrano de Bergerac   69

22. Just because you're an expert doesn't mean your opinion is right   71

23. You need to exaggerate to illustrate   73

24. A positive attitude can refocus your energy on the good in life   75

25. Laughter is the best medicine. No productive work will get done during an exceptionally lousy day.   77

26. Figure out how to compensate for your weaknesses   79

27. Figure out if you are a "Touch Wet Paint" person   81

28. In stressful moments, lean on your strengths   83

29. Sometimes, people don't always know when you're joking   85

30. Lay low, very low, in the weeds (Part III)   87

31. At work, don't come to me with problems; come to me with solutions to problems.   89

32. Distraction from learning is the key to learning   91

33. Do what you love but don't jeopardize anyone you love. Including yourself.   93

EXAM 2: A trespasser, a trap, a scream   95

C. Justice & Education: Facing Your Rubber Room   97
34. Life is fragile, so appreciate every day   99

35. There's no place like home   101

36. The arc of the moral universe is long, but it bends toward justice~Reverend Martin Luther King   103

37. Intelligence is wrapped in many packages   111

38. A gentle word of encouragement can last a lifetime   113

39. Know the consequences of regret   115

40. It's good to be the judge! (Part II)   117

41. By failing to prepare, you are preparing to fail. When you're finished changing, you're finished.~ Benjamin Franklin   123

42. Learn at your own pace. You'll get there eventually.   127

43. Never crush anyone's dreams   129

44. Find your Light Bulb Moment   131

FINAL EXAM: A rubber room, you, a scream   133

III. Graduation   135

Epilogue   143

Acknowledgements   147

About the Author   149

PROLOGUE

Rub·ber Room *(noun)*

A confining mind-set where thoughts and possibilities bounce aimlessly

Unlocking Your Rubber Room highlights the lessons I learned through trial and error as a lawyer and college professor. Using humor, the book explores how law and education play an integral role in unleashing your potential and dealing with everyday life. Some tips are funny, some are serious, and the obvious ones come to life through rich anecdotes. There are also whimsical observations sprinkled throughout, to see if you're really paying attention.

We all live in rubber rooms in one form or another, whether professionally or personally. But we also have choices in how we face everyday dilemmas. With optimism or cynicism. With hope or fear. With belly laughs or tears.

As you read through my lessons, please keep these two questions in mind:

- Do you take yourself too seriously?

- Do you actually know what you want out of life?

The stories in *Unlocking Your Rubber Room* apply to everyone and will ignite your passion to laugh, think, and act. Each lesson provides space to take class notes, as a way to examine how it can be applied to your own life.

Finally, my intent is to unlock your rubber room, not for you to escape it! *Unlocking Your Rubber Room* embraces lifelong learning rather than quick fix solutions, as the key to professional and personal growth. Emphasizing preparation, passion, and compassion, the book is divided into three sections:

A. *Law & Negotiation – Padding Your Rubber Room*

B. *Potpourri – Organizing Your Rubber Room*

C. *Justice & Education – Facing Your Rubber Room*

Sections A and B contain fast-paced, practical, and playful lessons about law and life. Section C is a provocative look at the United States justice system, and how we have a choice to make when facing injustice. We can decide to live in fear, or instead use our anger as a constructive motivating tool to think and act through any situation.

Laugh. Think. Act.

Registration is over. Court and class are now in session.

I – Orientation
Unlocking <u>My</u> Rubber Room

The beautiful thing about learning is that no one can take it away from you.

~ Blues musician B.B. King

I never dreamed of being a college professor. Does anybody?

As a child, I was convinced that I would be a professional basketball player. When it became obvious that my footwork wasn't quick enough, I figured I better get my brain to work a little harder. I graduated from high school at 16, college at 20, and law school at 23. I was on the fast track.

I always gave my teachers fits in school, as evidenced by grade school report cards:

- Second Grade: Improvement needed in self control

- Fourth Grade: Perry needs to exert more self control

- Sixth Grade: Perry needs to exercise better self control

Psychologists will tell you that the best predictor of future behavior is past behavior. How then, did this misfit wind up in a classroom, the very scene of his childhood transgressions?

At age 23, I was eager to start my law career. You couldn't contain my ambitious smile, as I pulled out of hometown New York City and drove to Miami Vice in my polished turbocharged flame throwing Pinto.

When I drove to work that first day, I arrived in style: A navy blue pin-striped suit, virgin leather shoes and briefcase, and a Bucherer wristwatch. I stood outside that freshly minted 55-story skyscraper and looked up not with wonder, but with a sense of clarity and purpose. When I opened the glass doors, all I could smell was new.

Just two years prior, I was a bloody mess. Literally. My bruised listless body lay on the side of a road, with a smashed head and two broken hands. I was losing consciousness at the age of 21. No lullabies, no sweet dreams, no foreseeable future. Lying in a ravine and praying for the cast of <u>ER</u> to show up wasn't my idea of a good time.

But that was two years ago. I now had fire and passion in my belly.

I confidently ascended the escalator to my firm's elevator bank, when a familiar sensation suddenly came over me.

All I could think at that moment:

"This is gonna suck."

The prior fall, the firm's recruiter wandered up to my law school in Buffalo for an initial round of interviews. That guy was NOT leaving the room until he gave me a second interview in the land of sunshine and Crockett and Tubbs. I hung onto his words like a gator on a meaty leg.

When I got to Miami for the interview, he walked me to his office window and told me to look across the street at the skyscraper under construction. He put his fatherly hand on my shoulder and said my office could be up there next fall. I was wined, dined, and drained by the time they dumped me off at my hotel at midnight.

I accepted a job offer starting the following fall. That bitter Buffalo winter was sweet. As I huddled under blankets in front of space heaters and the TV, all I could watch was the national weather reports.

After moving to Miami, I worked long hours as a business litigator, someone who goes to court when a dispute arises between companies. I traded the Pinto in for a jet black Celica and cruised down neon-lit Brickell Avenue each night after work. With the sun roof open, the balmy weather mixed with the manufactured breeze. This was my license to childishly mock the upcoming Buffalo winter.

In court, I looked like I was 11 - maybe 16 with a suit and tie. Most opposing counsel perceived my youthful appearance as an invitation to bully an unseasoned attorney. In one case, I was having a hard time with an old, heavyset lawyer, "Sal," who defended a company that owed my client several thousand dollars. In routine law cases, attorneys are allowed to seek information from the other side in the "discovery" phase of the suit. As was my typical practice, I sent a notice for the other side to produce documents so I could analyze them and prepare for a future deposition of the defendant.

Only, this guy played games and never produced the documents or made his client available for the latter's sworn statement. Each time we set the depo, they never appeared. Sal abused the discovery process, and we had to run to the judge to make the big man comply. This took several court appearances and wasted a lot of time and my client's money.

Finally, I got Sal into our huge conference room. You've seen them in the movies: garish artwork, an obscenely long mahogany table, and a million high back leather chairs all around. Joining me was the court reporter to transcribe the events, and "Larry," a law clerk attending the local law school.

To no one's surprise, Sal and his client walked in late. As Sal flung the documents at me, he barked: "Start the deposition!" I calmly told him that Larry and I needed some time to look over the docs before beginning. "Start the deposition or we're outta here!" Blah. Blah. Blah.

After more yelling and whining, we started the deposition, where the deponent must answer questions under oath. Sal objected to almost every question, and we went at it. Back and forth, up and down, your mother, my mother. Finally, he leaned across the massive table, stared me down and blathered:

"I've been in this business too long to be pushed around by a young punk like you."

Okay. This was getting good. The court reporter even worked it into the record. I guess I needed to say something, as I sniffed the leather on my chair:

"Yeah, you're right; you have been in this business too long and it's about time we clean it up!"

Not bad, I'm thinking. Maybe a 6 out of 10 on comebacks. Well, whatever I said, Sal just snapped. He forklifted that huge ol' body out of his high leather chair and started waddling around the long table, coming after me like the Penguin on Batman. He screamed along the way:

"I've never hit an attorney, but I'm gonna hit you now!"

The court reporter's smile widened, as she kept on typing.

Meanwhile, I just sat in my high back, half amused as Sal made his way towards me. Suddenly, Larry sprung out of his chair and jumped in front of me as Sal approached. Larry assumed the now famous *Karate Kid* Crane Technique stance to ward off this looney lawyer. Sal waved his fist, so Larry started flapping his wings.

Not much surprises me, but this one's way up there. I whispered to Larry: "Why the Crane?" "If done properly, no defense," he offered in his best Mr. Miyagi voice. I just turned to the court reporter and said:

"Let the record reflect that opposing counsel waddled halfway around the room and threatened me with verbal and physical violence." And that Larry's getting a good letter of recommendation from me. Okay, maybe he wasn't exactly in the Crane position, but they should really teach that move in law school. Wax on. Wax off.

Waddling Weasel Sal got the last laugh though. His shenanigans did the trick. He delayed the case long enough to throw his client into bankruptcy. My client didn't get a dime. As if I didn't already know it, the practice of law is a game. But the stakes are awfully high and personal.

Seeking a distraction from my day job, I started teaching part-time at a local community college. Before the first class, a nervous wave came over me. Who's the tougher audience, a cranky old Waddling Sal, or a roomful of young college students cranking out questions?

Eventually, I switched to teaching full-time. The Celica now had 100,000 miles on it and the sun roof no longer opened. The engine always overheated when the AC ran, so I had to blast the heat to cool the motor. I started dreaming of Buffalo winters and driving everywhere with the windows rolled down, like *Ace Ventura: Pet Detective*.

Then, I was energized by a new challenge to teach in Atlanta. This time around, I had a few more miles on my tread.

In the movie *City Slickers*, Billy Crystal goes on a cattle drive out west with some buddies, trying to get his old smile back. Feeling down about a demotion at work and confused with his place in life, he asks Jack Palance, the old and crusty cowboy guide named Curly, what the meaning of life is. Jack holds up a finger, saying just one thing is the secret to life. Excited, Billy asks what it is. To which the sage replies: "That's what you've got to figure out."

The following pages are a crash course lesson in my one thing.

II – 44 Lessons

A. Law & Negotiation: Padding Your Rubber Room

- Lesson 1 -

It's good to be the judge! (Part 1)

My classroom syllabus says: No legal advice questions!

I get telephone calls from students when it's too late – <u>after</u> they have a court date. You know how you get one call before you are hauled off to prison? Well, I got this call from "Steve":

"Perry, I'm in the DeKalb County Detention Center. Get me out of here!"

His voice trailed off as he was pulled away by the corrections officer. Steve was charged with reckless driving – going over 100 mph. Unfortunately, my students like to drive fast. Steve, a good student, hard worker, and funny man in class, was young and had long braided hair. And he had no attorney when he went up to the judge. That is a prescription for disaster. Though I don't condone rocket speed driving, the judge gave him an excessive sentence of ten days in jail. So I drove to the detention center which is located along a busy street with fast food joints dotted throughout. As I pulled up to the building, I imagined the inmates banging on their little rectangular windows demanding freedom. Or at the very least, a cheeseburger.

It's 10:00 p.m., and they only let attorneys in to see clients at that time. The problem is that Steve's not my client. And I'm not a member of the Georgia Bar. So I whipped out a yellowing Florida Bar card and two box tops from Wheaties and told the guard that Steve is my student. After going through a ton of red tape, I got to see him. They put me in a little room facing glass, while they brought Steve in across from me. He was handcuffed and in his orange jumpsuit. I placed the palm of my hand on the glass and spread my fingers apart, because I saw that done on the TV prison show <u>Oz</u>. Steve smiled and put his hand up to mine. I gazed at my digits mirroring his across the glass and said to myself: "Hey, this TV hand thing actually works!"

I referred him to a criminal attorney who got him out of jail after three lousy nights. If Steve had an attorney at his first hearing, he never would've seen the inside of a jail. He showed up to court on time, but committed the crimes of being young, funny, without counsel, and clueless on what a judge can do. Welcome to the legal system as I know it. A good attorney will get respect from the bench that the average citizen might not. A judge has wide discretion on sentencing and it helps to have one's own advocate.

Don't call me! Get a lawyer! I've seen judges walk into court late and apologize for wasting everyone's time. But if you are late to court or catch a judge in the wrong mood, you can be held in contempt, fined, and even jailed.

Always remember: It's good to be the judge!

Another time, a student's mom called me to bail her daughter out of jail. "Alice" spent the night in jail for being a passenger in a reportedly stolen car. When she walked into the holding cell where I was waiting, I gave her two options.

"Either I could bail you out now…"

"Yes, YES, let's go!"

"Or… (as I reached into my briefcase and pulled out some papers) … you can take the Midterm exam you missed last week."

"Get me the freak outta here!"

Always remember: It's good to be the teacher!

- Lesson 2 -

Finding leverage is the key to enforcing a contract

Class hypothetical: Sally went into a car dealer one evening and signed a contract to purchase a truck. When she expressed her hesitancy to sign the contract, the dealer closed the deal by saying to her: "Drive the truck around for a week; if you still have doubts, come back and we'll cancel the deal." Sally had no witnesses to this statement. She went back to the dealer the next morning, regretting the amount of money that the truck will cost. Of course, the dealer said that she couldn't get out of the contract.

The dealer gets to stand on a standard clause in the contract which would exclude the statement made by the dealer to the buyer. However, the statement was still a misrepresentation of fact - leading to several legal claims including fraud. But where's our witness? How can we prove this in court?

Unless the written agreement states that you have a certain number of days to cancel the contract, you need to assume that you cannot get out of it. A consumer in this scenario should immediately turn to state and federal consumer statutes to see if there are any remedies.

Does Sally have leverage in this case to get out of the deal? Probably not, but what could she do?

When trapped in a bad deal, I believe in creating leverage. Leverage in this situation is obviously created when armed with an attorney. However, not everyone has that luxury. The next step is to get a consumer advocate working for you, and as a last resort, taking your case to the media. The dealer might want to avoid the bad publicity and work it out. Otherwise, I'm afraid that Sally will have little or no recourse.

Final Note: Sally better be correct in any assertion to the media, because this kind of action can lead to a slander lawsuit by the dealer.

Leverage is the determining factor for writing a good contract that the other side will sign. If the other side "needs the deal" more than we do, we'll have leverage in the negotiations. If there is ever a contract dispute, hopefully the language we negotiate will back us up. Leverage comes in many forms, and it usually comes down to money.

A cynical comment - Contracts are sometimes made to be broken. Just because parties signed on the dotted line, it doesn't mean all is well. If business people sign a bad deal and are losing money, they might try to get out of the deal. If the other side does not agree, some business people will consider breaching the contract to force a more reasonable arrangement. If that person has a bigger "war chest" (more money) than the person wishing to enforce the deal, that translates into leverage and possibly a favorable deal.

- Lesson 3 -

In deal making, make the other side feel like a hero

In a good negotiation, the goal is not to beat the other side into submission. If the leverage is clearly on your side, I guess you have the opportunity to do so, but this tact will cause resentment down the road if you have dealings with the same person. When leverage is on an equal playing field, the goal for getting a deal done should be to get both sides what they want. When you benefit from a deal and the other side feels good about it, you may have begun a long term business relationship which could bear even greater fruit.

An extreme analogy to illustrate this hero point is the Cuban Missile Crisis. In 1962, the world was on the brink of nuclear war when Soviet General Secretary Nikita Khrushchev authorized the building of missile bases in Cuba, just off U.S. shores. When President Kennedy ordered a blockade of Soviet ships carrying weapons to Cuba, the leaders conducted secret ongoing negotiations. Eventually the Soviets relented, withdrawing the weapons and dismantling the missile bases. Kennedy gained instant respect worldwide, while Khrushchev was embarrassed by his alleged weakness. Unknown at the time though was that the deal hinged on the United States agreeing to dismantle its own missile base in Turkey, along the Soviet Union's border. Had Khrushchev been able to claim an immediate victory for the Turkey deal, he could've "saved face" in the crisis aftermath, and possibly even be viewed as a hero to his country. Instead, he was out of office within two years, and relations between the two powers remained tense for decades.

Business deals should be a little easier to manage than superpower negotiations. Simply put, if you make the other side look like heroes to the people who hold them accountable, they are more likely to do business with you again.

- Lesson 4 -

Stay home! Don't go to work!!

Everything is a lawsuit waiting to happen. We see all of these wacky cases in the paper:

1. A 19 year old won $74,000 and medical expenses when his neighbor ran over his hand while backing out of a driveway. The teenager apparently didn't notice that there was someone at the wheel of the car when he was trying to steal the neighbor's hubcaps.

2. While driving, a man placed a milkshake between his legs, leaned over to reach into his bag of food, and squeezed the milkshake container in the process. This action distracted the driver, causing him to hit another car. The man sued the drive-through restaurant for failing to warn him against eating while driving.

3. A restaurant was ordered to pay $113,500 to a woman who slipped on a soft drink and broke her coccyx bone. The drink was on the floor because the woman flung it at her boyfriend during an argument, 30 seconds earlier.

(FYI - #1 & #3 are urban legends making the rounds on the internet)

My tongue-in-cheek advice to students is that if they wish to avoid legal trouble, they better stay home and get under the covers because there's legal liability out there at every turn…

Stay home! Don't go to work!! Don't get in your car! Place warnings on all products! Offer anger management training for customers! Don't turn on your computer! Do not look at or speak to anyone!

- Lesson 5 -

Always have a sandwich bag, a cell phone, and a big mouth

You're munching on a salad and you bite down hard into a strange object which happens to be a fish hook. As blood is gushing and your tooth is aching, what should you do?

The waiter is always trained to help get rid of the evidence:

"Oh my gosh! I'll be back with another salad, let me have that one and yank that lawsuit from your mouth. I am SO sorry. Please, let dinner be on us."

They got you. Hook. Salad bar line. Lawsuit sinker.

With bloody tongue-in-cheek, my students now know that they must carry two essential items and possess one vital skill when dining out:

1.   a plastic sandwich bag

2.   a cell phone

3.   a loud voice

The baggy is for the fish hook. Bag that evidence! If a cut leads to infection or if you damage your teeth, you can help your attorney by preserving the evidence. Isn't it easier for prosecutors to win a murder case when they find the body?

The cell phone is for two things. If you're seriously injured, of course call for an ambulance if you need immediate medical attention. If not, quickly take a picture or video of the hook, your bloody mouth, the shocked look on the waiter's face, and all of the witnesses who heard you scream and watched you extract the hook. It's another piece of valuable evidence and proof.

The loud voice is for:

1. making sure the world knows you're injured. "I'm hurt. I'm hurt!"

2. obtaining witness names and telephone numbers

3. putting the restaurant manager on notice that you're injured

4. ensuring that days later, you do not speak on the telephone with anyone who tries to get you to admit that you're feeling okay, whether it's the concerned restaurant manager or an insurance company. You never know who's taping something. The restaurant is trying to build a defense against you, sitting there suffering from hook in mouth disease, by saying that you weren't really hurt. Just get off the phone quickly by referring them to your own insurance company or attorney.

Sandwich Bag. Cell Phone. Big Mouth. Now go enjoy your peaceful and serene dining experience. And re-read Lesson 4.

- Lesson 6 -

Buying a car from a dealer is like a New York City street fight

It's you against three in a dark alley. You know you're going down, but you better take one of them down with you. Recognize that you'll be taken in some form or another in the car buying negotiation, no matter how prepared you are. But don't make it easy for them.

A student once came up to me after class and said she bought a new car, only to discover that she actually had leased the vehicle. She realized this error weeks after the purchase, when she received her payment booklet in the mail. On the contract, the word "Lease" appeared at the top, rather than "Finance Agreement" or "Security Agreement." I sent her right back to the dealer that day, armed will all sorts of legal arguments and the threat to use her big mouth to scare off customers (see Lesson 5). Luckily they tore up the lease and replaced it with a finance agreement at the same payment terms.

I don't know if she struck a good deal, but you can't make it that easy for dealers to take you down. At least make sure that one of them goes down with you.

- Lesson 7 -

How to get a lawyer to return your call

The number one complaint against most attorneys is lack of communication with their clients. In fact, lawyers can be sanctioned by the state bar if the transgression is serious enough.

The best way to get an attorney on the phone is to tell the receptionist that you have a new client to refer to the lawyer. That gets 'em on the phone real fast, but it'll only work one time.

- Lesson 8 -

Lay low, very low, in the weeds (Part 1)

Don't bug a landlord for the return of a security deposit just after you vacate the premises at the end of a rental lease. In my state, tenants can get their security deposit back in its entirety from a landlord who owns ten or more units, if that landlord doesn't send the money or a letter detailing all of the damages in a timely manner. So don't call your landlord for the deposit until after that time period expires! Look up your state law and lay low in the weeds.

- Lesson 9 -

Getting too lawyered up can leave you with nothing

While attorneys are critical to protecting your rights, sometimes they propose overkill. Lawyers are worst-case scenario thinkers who can "gum up the works" for a business person.

For example, if an inventor seeks legal protection for an invention, it usually takes between one to five years before a patent application is granted by the United States Patent and Trademark Office (USPTO). During that time period, the application can be held in confidence by the USPTO for up to eighteen months, with a number of exceptions. In the interim, the inventor has the option of developing, marketing, and selling the invention while affixing a "patent pending" label. What patent pending does is put the public on notice that someone has applied for the patent and, if granted, can file a lawsuit against those who infringe on it during the patent pending period (say that fast three times). Remedies include suing for royalties, seizure of infringing items, and an injunction against further copying.

However, during the patent pending period, anyone who sees the new product can copy it, manufacture it, and make a pretty penny off of it before the inventor can assert legal rights. Thus, an extremely cautious attorney might have a client wait up to eighteen months before unveiling a product, to see if they can somehow get the patent granted within the confidential application window. However, most entrepreneurial clients need to move a product to market well before that time frame and are willing to face the risks.

Each situation is different, and while the legal advice may be prudent, it is up to business people to figure out where to draw the line and decide whether to tell their lawyers to shut up!

- Lesson 10 -

Sometimes your mother is all you really need

If the other side in a dispute or negotiation is being unreasonable, hard-headed, and a jerk, "Your Mother!" is an eloquent and dignified way of expressing yourself. It cuts quite swiftly to your point.

Be advised though that you're now likely heading down the road to a court-house war.

- Lesson 11 -

Nothing is funny in law

True case: A restaurant manager held a contest - whoever sells the most beer in one month will win a Toyota. Armed with that incentive, a waitress went tunnel vision to sell product. At the end of the month, she won the contest. To make the prize presentation dramatic, the manager blindfolded her and led her into the parking lot where the whole wait staff and the car awaited. As the blindfold came off and the waitress looked around for the Toyota, all she saw was the manager holding a toy Yoda doll.

Not funny to the waitress, who was thinking:

"You keep the doll; I'm calling a lawyer."

She sued the restaurant for the car. It may not have been a formal contract because her job was to serve beer anyway. However, there is a legal concept called "promissory estoppel," which says: She relied on a promise to her detriment and was harmed.

The case settled for an undisclosed amount, proving that nothing is funny in law!

- Lesson 12 -

Just because it's legal, doesn't mean it's moral

The goal of most people is to act within the bounds of the law. It is a matter of whose perspective you are considering to determine if laws and court rulings are fair.

From 1984-1988, a manufacturer was given $13.5 million in tax abatements to keep its Willow Run plant in the state of Michigan. In 1991, the company announced that it was closing the plant and moving its operations to Texas. The closure meant the loss of thousands of jobs and financial difficulties for the city, which did not have an express contract with the company. The city filed a lawsuit alleging promissory estoppel: "We gave you abatements in reliance on your promise to stay." But stay for how long? The appellate court ruled that any statements made by the manufacturer were mere expressions of hope or expectation, but did not amount to a promise.

In the practice of law, there is a continual tension and interplay among business people, attorneys, and morality. It was up to the city to express terms for giving a tax break. The company's actions made good business sense, but did these actions pass moral muster? Regardless, something may be legal, but not necessarily moral.

- Lesson 13 -

Lay low, very low, in the weeds (Part II)

Every semester, I ask my students if they've ever lent money to a boyfriend, girlfriend, or family member, but never got repaid. Lots of hands go up. Then with trepidation, I ask if anyone ever heard the scariest words on the planet: "If you love me."

"If you love me, you'll loan me more money."

"If you love me, you'll co-sign this loan."

"If you love me, you'll pull that bank job."

If you hear those four words, dive headfirst into the weeds.

- Lesson 14 -

Sometimes, life can be murder. Or not.

The State of Georgia legislature passed the following bill:

Right to Self-Defense Act
*A person is justified in threatening or using force against another <u>and does
not have a duty to retreat</u> when and to the extent that he or she reasonably
believes that such threat or force is necessary to defend himself or herself or a
third person against such other's imminent use of unlawful force.*

This is the Shoot First law. The key change in the law is the underlined
portion above, eliminating the need to retreat from another person's force if one
is able to. In other words, people can stand their ground and meet reasonably
perceived deadly force with their own deadly force.

Hypothetical: You're in a city park in the daylight hours and there is a
person 200 feet away. He is limping slowly towards you with a walking cane in
one hand and a big old axe in the other. He yells: "I'm gonna cut you up and feed
you to the pigeons." You are wearing your running shoes and happen to be on

the university track team. You also happen to lawfully possess an Uzi machine gun on your person.

Most states have a self defense law which dictates that you have a duty to try and retreat, if possible, when facing deadly force – not to stand your ground and meet this force with your own deadly force.

So in my hypothetical, you better haul on out of there. However, if there is no duty to retreat, I guess that the possibilities are endless:

You: Well hello there, Mr. Limping Crazy Man wielding a lumberman's axe. Your blade looks mighty sharp and shiny.

Him: Why yes, better to slice you to ribbons.

You: Hang on a second as I record this scenario on my video cell phone.

Him: Did they give you a rebate on that phone? Hey, by the way, my name is Johnny. Heeeeeeeere's Johnny!

You: Great. Come a step closer. And by the way, say hello to my little semi-automatic friend!

If zealous district attorneys wish to prosecute you, they'll need to show that you did not act reasonably. What do the phrases "reasonably believe" or "imminent use of unlawful force" mean in the above law? That's a question of fact for the jury as to whether your act constituted homicide. Or as I like to say, "Muuuurrrrder."

- Lesson 15 -

Company lawyers think we are really stupid

I found this on the internet so it must be true:

Funny (But Actual) Product Warnings

Instructions for hairdryer	Do not use while sleeping
On a kitchen knife	Keep out of children
On a clothing iron	Do not iron clothes on body *
On a package of peanuts	Warning: Contains nuts
On a chainsaw	Do not attempt to stop chain with your hands

* Admit it – you've done this, or at least thought about it!

EXAM 1:
A car, a coffee, a scream

This morning on the way to our exam, Marcel purchased coffee at the drive-through window of a local burger establishment. With the car stopped, he placed the cup between his knees and opened the lid to add cream. Accidentally, he knocked the contents of the cup onto his lap, and hot coffee soaked through his sweat pants. He screamed: "Help me, I'm burning, and I've got a test in 20 minutes!" After completing his exam, Marcel headed straight to the hospital, where doctors treated his third degree burns. He then sued the burger joint for failing to warn him that extremely hot coffee can rip through flesh. A jury awarded Marcel $100,000 in compensatory damages, but also found him to be 75% responsible and the defendant 25% responsible for the accident.

How much money would Marcel be permitted to recover if the defendant does not appeal this verdict?

a. $100,000

b. $75,000

c. $25,000

d. $0

If you chose letter "c," then you understand the legal concept of comparative negligence. In most states, a plaintiff's award is reduced by the percentage of fault assigned by the jury for an accident. However, in my state, if a plaintiff is found to be 50% or more responsible, then that plaintiff would recover nothing from the $100,000 verdict. Thus, the correct response would be letter "d." Tricky, but this question highlights the importance of knowing your state laws.

II – 44 Lessons

B. Potpourri:
Organizing Your Rubber Room

- Lesson 16 -

Sometimes you need to suck it up and wing it

One day, I was sleepwalking through the airport at 9:00 a.m. There was a crying little kid next to me and a mom screaming: "We're all gonna die!" My boy. My wife. Oh joy. With the first class of the semester a mere six hours and 600 miles away, I'd know by 4:15 p.m. if 120 students were collectively thinking: "This professor sucks!"

We had spent five days in Florida with the folks, where my two year old, Kevin, tore up the joint. It's quite the serene moment when your child screams the whole night, then flight, because you won't let him push the overhead emergency light button for an hour straight. And your spouse is convinced that the plane will be deposited into the ocean shortly after takeoff.

The first day of class is always the most important day of the semester because it sets the tone for the course. I was off to a compelling start.

We landed in Atlanta on time. As the wife and kid headed home by car, I jumped on the train to campus. By 3:00 p.m., I was exhausted from lack of sleep, the flight, flashing button lights, and apocalyptic predictions of plane malfunctions. But for an hour and 15 minutes, I needed to summon up the energy to keep people alive. It's the last class of the day for most students, so I was what stood between them and Oprah at 4:00 p.m. Now THAT is pressure.

So I sucked it up, winged it, and crashed after class.

- Lesson 17 -

Know the consequences of no regrets

I had a student who said there was a "pie in the sky" casting call, but it meant getting in line and waiting for hours at a downtown hotel. And missing my class. I simply told her that she could go, but was responsible for getting class notes from a fellow student. I'm a big believer in going after opportunities, even when it means sometimes doing the irresponsible thing, like telling a professor that you need to ditch class for a pipe dream of a chance at something big.

I learned that lesson when, as a law student, I was clerking at the U.S. Attorney's Office, a great place to learn about government law. A movie was being filmed downtown starring Robert Redford, and they needed extras to fill up an old minor league baseball stadium. I really wanted to go, thinking it would be fun, but instead I did the responsible thing by going to work that day. Years later, every time I see *The Natural*, one of my favorite all-time sports movies, I say to myself if only I called in sick that day.

Thankfully, this is a minor regret, but it served as a lesson to me about professional risk taking and understanding the consequences.

Be a risk taker, but know where to draw the foul line.

- Lesson 18 -

Figure out if you are a "structure" person or someone who can self-motivate at any given time

I like a little bit of structure, but not too much. Classes bring that framework to my work life. A long time ago, I did some full-time freelance work and found it difficult to motivate myself day in and day out. In that environment, you have to create a regimen and stick to it with discipline. For me, just knowing that I need to be at a certain place on time brings me certainty, clarity, and anticipation.

- Lesson 19 -

Your computer's "spell check" is not the same as proofreading

In a legal document, an attorney asked the judge for a delay in his case because he was undergoing a delicate medical procedure on his back: Disk surgery. However, he mistakenly typed a different four letter word that looked like DISK, inserting an unfortunate "C" rather than the needed "S."

Spell check didn't pick up the error, since the word was spelled correctly. The result: Every lawyer I know got an e-mailed copy of that document.

- Lesson 20 -

Why not us?

Great things happen because you make them happen. We are not <u>entitled</u> to success and happiness. But if we go after them full force, why not us?

- Lesson 21 -

Sometimes we all need a Cyrano de Bergerac

Before I knew that my wife was pregnant with our second kid, she walked in the room one morning with a big smile, while holding a little white stick. I've seen that thing before. The pregnancy stick.

She handed it to me and pointed to the part with two crossed blue lines to indicate a positive result. After a big hug, I'm thinking, what do you say in one of these moments? They always get it so right and perfect in the movies. Digging deep down into my Reservoir of Smooth, I offered my sweet wife:

"By the way honey, which end of the pee stick am I holding?"

- Lesson 22 -

Just because you're an expert doesn't mean your opinion is right

A long time ago, I was taking a college film course for fun. On the first day of that class, the professor went around the room asking people what their favorite movie was. I said *GoodFellas*, which I boldly predicted would be considered the greatest movie made in the 90's. I thought my position was defensible since director Martin Scorsese received similar critical acclaim for *Raging Bull*, which many consider the best movie of the 80's. That professor shot me a look and proceeded to tell me that my opinion was ridiculous.

I kept my unflattering thoughts to myself. Your mother!

Okay, I made my prediction before *Saving Private Ryan*, *Schindler's List*, and *Forrest Gump* came out, but I felt vindicated in the late 1990's when the American Film Institute listed *GoodFellas* as one of the top 100 movies of the century.

My point here – don't treat people with disrespect, even if you think their opinions are dumb. They aren't right or wrong if it's just an opinion.

- Lesson 23 -

You need to exaggerate to illustrate

Learning and retaining dense information isn't all about laughter, though it helps. For class, I comb the internet each day for wacky law cases. After a while, I can sense which stuff gets the best laughs. Like a comic working in a club testing out new material, I constantly work on delivery, timing, and audience engagement. However, the use of exaggeration in a classroom or boardroom is not about telling jokes. In fact, I can recall telling only one joke in class:

"What's the only thing worse than biting into an apple and finding a worm?"

"Finding half a worm!"

And that's why I stay away from joke telling.

Exaggeration is the secret to effective learning. It requires me to plant a picture so implausible and outlandish in the learners' minds, that they can't help but remembering the concept. For an example, think back to Lesson 14, about self-defense to the charge of Muuuurrrrder.

I believe that storytelling is a learnable skill, as demonstrated in the movie, *Reservoir Dogs*. In a few scenes, an undercover detective tirelessly trains a colleague on the fine art of spinning a tale. The key, he explains, is in remembering and exploiting the story's rich details.

Finally, in the spirit of "less is truly more," all you need is a headline to spark a collective imagination of where the next lesson is going:

MAN SUES HIMSELF FOR HITTING HIS OWN CAR

- Lesson 24 -

A positive attitude can refocus your energy on the good in life

My favorite quote is from Bud Greenspan, the Olympic filmmaker and historian. In response to a letter I wrote him about politics and corruption in the Olympic movement, he offered: "I'd still rather spend 100% of the time on the 90% that's good – than 100% of my time on the 10% that's not so good."

When cynicism creeps into my bones from time to time, I try to remember that positive attitude.

- Lesson 25 -

Laughter is the best medicine. No productive work will get done during an exceptionally lousy day.

I always dread giving back the first exam of the semester since it's the first time students might get bad news or feedback. So after going over the test, we usually take a break, and I need to use my best material.

I start off by asking the class: "Who here's ever been to a pawn shop?" But I ask in my New York accent, because the word "pawn" in New Yorkese sounds like "porn."

"Who here has been to a 'porn' shop?"

Three hands shoot up from the back row – three guys – yeah, me! Uneasiness and mild laughter follows.

"Come on, who here's been in a 'porn' shop?"

Disbelief and murmurs all around. Finally, someone's smart enough to ask in a proper Southern accent: "Do you mean a paaaaaaaawn, shop?"

"Yeah, a 'porn' shop." (playing innocent)

Raucous laughter fills the room.

"What?"

"It's paaaaaaaawn shop."

Then they ask how I say porn and pawn.

"Porn. And porn."

Then we go on to discuss a case dealing with contracts and a paaaaaaaawn shop. The day still stinks, but it's a little lighter.

- Lesson 26 -

Figure out how to compensate for your weaknesses

One of my glaring weaknesses as a professor is an inability to remember student names or recognize their faces outside of class. One time in class, a student walked up to me and said: "I saw you on campus yesterday, and you didn't even say 'hi'. That was rude!" I desperately tried to explain that names and faces are hard for me to recall on a huge campus.

So now, when I walk around a campus of 30,000 students, I'm compelled to wave hello to everyone I make contact with. "Hi, how goes it?!" or "Hope you're doing well." Four out of five of them are looking at me, like: "Do I know you?" or "Who the heck are you!?" But that fifth person, the one I should know, appreciates the hello. So I'm walking, smiling, waving, and babbling. All over campus. It's either that, or stare at my feet as I plow towards the lecture hall.

- Lesson 27 -

Figure out if you are a "Touch Wet Paint" person

What kind of kid were you growing up? The kind that respected a wet paint sign, or one that found it so irresistible that you had to touch it? The decision to touch or not touch highlights whether you are a curious person or someone who believes everything you read. Or someone who just acts on impulse.

I was showing a video in class and the students wanted me to turn out the lights in the front. Not knowing how to work the lights, I hit all of the switch buttons. Nothing worked. I had no clue. Finally, I saw a switch which was covered over in white adhesive tape, with the obvious implied message that cried out: "Don't touch this, you idiot!"

I did. The overhead projector and everything else electric in the room suddenly went dead.

This professor sucks!

- Lesson 28 -

In stressful moments, lean on your strengths

I learned this lesson in the first class I ever taught, Introduction to American Government.

I thought that we should begin at the very beginning of the text, with a discussion of the Founding Fathers and the Federalist Papers. As I started talking, I repeatedly said to myself: "You don't know anything about this topic beyond what you read last night." After forty five minutes of panic, sweat, and utter confusion, we took a 10 minute break. In that time, I decided to go straight to the Bill of Rights, a topic of strength. The rest of the session went very smoothly.

- Lesson 29 -

Sometimes, people don't always know when you're joking

Sample questions my students have asked me during class:

- Are you a member of an organized crime family?

- Are you really in the witness protection program?

- Have you ever killed someone?

- Why do hot dogs come in packs of 10 and buns in packs of 8?

- Lesson 30 -

Lay low, very low, in the weeds (Part III)

The jewelry industry likes to apply marketing pressure on those in love to spend three months salary or more on engagement rings. Recently, I read that the Gemological Institute of America has seen a 41 percent jump in the number of two-carat-plus diamonds that it processes since 2000. TWO carats. Plus. Ouch!

One semester, a student told the class about a friend who bought a diamond ring for his future fiancée, with the intent of proposing on a camping trip. The guy picked a romantic, tender moment to give the love of his life this special ring. As he got down on his knee and produced this glittering rock, his loving girlfriend eagerly looked at it, then screamed: "This isn't the &%@* diamond I wanted!," and threw the ring. Into the woods! Your mother!

The guy searched for over an hour and luckily found his symbol of love. I don't know if they stayed engaged, and I never give personal advice in class. In this case, I made an exception:

"Guys, if this happens to you, run! Don't even look back for the ring. Run fast from this Blair Witch!"

And next time propose in a sealed hyperbaric chamber.

- Lesson 31 -

At work, don't come to me with problems; come to me with solutions to problems.

I learned this lesson on the job when I went to my boss about a problem on a law case. He just yelled at me to come back to him with some ways to get out of the dilemma.

A good boss or manager:

- does not want to micromanage employees,
- knows that problems pop up at work, and
- dislikes headaches.

It is more refreshing for your supervisor to hear from you: "There's a problem with this account, but I figured out a few ways to fix it. Can I run them by you if you have a moment?"

Conversely, I believe that managers shouldn't waste their team members' time by asking for input on a decision when that decision has already been made. Sometimes, bosses do this to create an environment of inclusion or to get a pulse on the imminent reaction to the decision. For me, better to have no input than to have the illusion of input at work.

- Lesson 32 -

Distraction from learning is the key to learning

The classroom gives me freedom to do things I couldn't do in a courtroom – be myself. In class, if I want to jump on a table, scream out the door, or answer a student's cell phone, it not only is acceptable, but is happily taken in by the class. I wonder if a judge would appreciate this behavior.

I like an atmosphere of expecting the unexpected. I actually welcome distractions and discovered that they help students retain material. When their minds are wandering, I need something to bring them back on track.

At the review for my first exam, students are typically very nervous, not really knowing what to expect on the test. To break the tension, I'll give my chalk or marker to a student sitting in the middle of the room. As I run back to the front of the classroom, I implore the student to stand up and wing it at my head! Some respectful students wouldn't think of committing a battery on their professor, until egged on by rowdy classmates.

I've been nailed only one time in all these years. And now let's get back to the review.

- Lesson 33 -

Do what you love but don't jeopardize anyone you love. Including yourself.

Recognize and assess the risks in every major decision you make. And how they affect those around you.

When I left the full-time practice of law to teach, I was single and had no children. Would I have made such a career transition if I had a spouse and two kids at the time? I'd like to think so because in the end, career satisfaction is one key to personal fulfillment. Some opportunities are rare and don't come around often. The difficult part is learning whether to jump at or pass on an adventure when your responsibilities require the support of those around you and a closer look at risk and reward.

EXAM 2:
A trespasser, a trap, a scream

Harold Homeowner didn't like having the neighborhood teenagers walk across his yard every night. So he dug a huge hole on his lawn, along the path these people usually take. Then he placed a bear trap at the bottom of the hole and cleverly covered it with small branches and leaves. One night while walking across Harold's property, Tim fell in, got caught in the bear trap, and was seriously injured. The next morning, Harold went out for the newspaper and to see what he'd caught. Tim screamed: "My leg. I'm hurt!" In Tim's lawsuit for injuries, Harold will likely:

a. win because Tim was a trespasser and landowners owe no duty to trespassers. Harold could even surround his home with a mote filled with water and alligators to make sure Tim stays off his freshly cut lawn.

b. lose because landowners owe a duty to keep the premises free from unreasonable dangers they create for trespassers.

I know which answer you'd like to pick. Choose the other one for exam purposes.

II — 44 Lessons

C. Justice & Education: Facing Your Rubber Room

- Lesson 34 -

Life is fragile, so appreciate every day

For the past year, I've kept a judge's business card taped to my computer screen. Judge Rowland was one of the good judges. He was considered fair and compassionate by attorneys, and I was lucky enough to have him as a guest speaker in my class. The students loved interacting with him and it was less intimidating for them to see a judge out of his black robe, in everyday clothing.

Rowland didn't retire or go back to private practice. No, he was gunned down while sitting on the bench when a man on trial for rape got a deputy's gun, killed one deputy, wounded another, and killed a court reporter and a federal agent. And assassinated Rowland. The judge is survived by a spouse and daughter.

A widow. A fatherless girl. And a monster.

.

- Lesson 35 -

There's no place like home

A few years ago, I met a person who was the victim of unfortunate circumstances. After five years of home ownership, his mortgage lender stated that there was an unpaid balance in the escrow account and started to wrongfully apply mortgage payments to this alleged amount owed. After four months of arguing about the error and falling behind in payments, the bank began foreclosure proceedings against the homeowner. He then foolishly gave money equaling two mortgage payments to a foreclosure consultant firm. The company did nothing, he was out that money, and subsequently out on the street. To compound the problem, he was ineligible for public assistance, since his credit report incorrectly indicated assets from the sale of the home! The story does have a happy ending, as he got back on his feet and into school.

When you think things like that can't happen to you, consider this case.

In Miami, I went into a homeless shelter as part of a volunteer legal aid program, where someone with a legal problem could speak with an attorney. I met a guy there who was arrested and thrown in jail on a case of mistaken identity. The man had a very stable lifestyle before his arrest, paying rent to the same landlord for twenty years. In addition, he had enough money in the bank to pay a lawyer. But he sat in prison for months while his lawyer did nothing. With no family unit to support him, the man's landlord never got a rent check, so the latter commenced eviction proceedings. All of the guy's possessions were put out on the street. When he was finally able to show that it was a case of mistaken identity, he had no home, no money, and no possessions.

Circumstances and lack of family structure can lead to some scary places. He was referred to legal aid for assistance.

- Lesson 36 -

The arc of the moral universe is long, but it bends toward justice
~Reverend Martin Luther King

There's no place like home.
There's no place like home.
There's no place like home.

The great thing about knowing how to work the court system is that you can help people out in times of crisis. The worst thing though is that sometimes you witness too much grief. People usually come to attorneys in vulnerable moments of crisis and when one sees that every day, he or she tends to get a jaded view of the world. After Hurricane Katrina, for example, most people didn't have government issued flood insurance. Even if they did, it might not have been enough to rebuild. But was it flooding or a storm surge caused by hurricane winds which sent water into everyone's home? What the heck is the difference? Plenty, and that's the multibillion dollar coverage question. Many insurance companies took the formal legal position of: "Uh, we don't think so." So that issue will be litigated into the next decade while displaced homeowners can't rebuild.

As attorneys argue in court for years over property damages, I fret for the mental health of each affected survivor, especially the kids. A while back, I saw a newspaper article on the trauma of disasters like Katrina, and it mentioned the case studies done in Buffalo Creek, West Virginia.

In the early 1970's, Buffalo Creek was a peaceful coal mining town. To make coal commercially saleable, the company had to wash and separate the coal from surrounding rock, soil, and impurities. This process produces waste or sludge or "slurry," which needs to be put somewhere, so why not put the nasty stuff in running streams or babbling brooks. And impound the stuff by constructing dams upstream from the valley where miners and their families live.

The first dam built by the mining company was about ten feet high and it must have been built by beavers because the mining people quickly realized they needed a bigger dam, so they built one further upstream which was twenty feet high, and I'm guessing that business and production was good, because more refuse was dumped into the impounded water, so the company decided to build a dam further upstream, reaching sixty feet high and 450 feet wide. Hot damn.

One year later, a lesson in physics. What happens when you have a dam with black sludge contained close to the top? And it rains. And rains. And keeps raining. Meanwhile, the people monitoring the height of the dam were doing so not with a water gauge, but with a fancy stick at the edge of the water, looking for marks. And ten months prior to this moment, the state Department of Natural Resources told the company that the dam needed an emergency spillway or overflow. The water just kept rising on a Thursday. Even though the guy looking at the water on Friday determined that the level was receding, and made this conclusion without even looking at the divining rod in the ground. And that night, the other guy who put the stick in the water went back to check and was startled to discover that the first guy was terribly wrong. The water hadn't receded. It had risen eighteen inches from the prior night!

The stick guy had the sense enough to stay there all night watching the magic wand. Well, then he saw that the water was a foot from the top of the dam and that it was rising three inches an hour! And no one in the valley down below had been told to get the heck out of Dodge. So at 5:00 o'clock Saturday morning, stick guy calls and wakes up the other guy who happens to be in charge, and says: "Get the freak down here!" or something to that effect. Decision man gets up but first stops off at the coffee shop for his usual cup. He bumps into the town sheriff there, who tags along as they get to the dam at 6:00 a.m. The sheriff stroked his beard and said that he was thinking about calling in the National Guard. Decision man checked in with corporate first. So at 7:30 a.m., he called the sheriff after conferring with the office about the status of the dam. Decision man assured the sheriff that everything was alright and the dam was under control. Thirty minutes later the dam broke. And nobody had warned the people in the valley! All of the miners were at home asleep with their families because Saturday wasn't a work day.

Oops. Oompa. Damn dam.

Anyone who's gone rafting or canoeing knows the fury of rushing water. Add on top of that the violent rush of once contained water. And if you can bear the thought, water mixed with unimaginable dark gunk. Over 130 million gallons of water and stuff. A bit different from the spring water delivered to your home in five gallon jugs. As the valley dwellers below slept, this angry water swept them and their cheaply built houses away. Away.

125 dead. 1,000 homes destroyed. 4,000 survivors dealing with the aftermath.

This horror story is recounted in graphic detail in Gerald Stern's book, *The Buffalo Creek Disaster*. The accounts of survivors are chilling. The one that I can't get out of my head is of a family - a pregnant mother named Gladys, a dad named Rowland, and their two year old - who made their way to the roof of the house, clinging on for dear life as the water level rose and became more furious. Finally, as Gladys was losing her grip, she looked into Rowland's eyes. Her last words in the madness: "Take care of my baby." Gladys and her unborn child were washed away and buried beneath the sludge. Rowland held his son tightly and held onto the home, but he was thrashed around so much that he lost his kid. "I lost that boy of mine. I don't know where." The little boy's name was Kevin, same as my own two year old. And he was gone.

Two hours of a full force tidal wave over seventeen miles through sixteen communities in Buffalo Creek Valley. In a maddening rush, I started thinking about that judge named Rowland who had been shot dead in his courtroom, and I tried to compare the incomparable of losing your own life and having your own family grieve for you, versus Buffalo Creek Rowland living through a tragedy and witnessing the destruction of his entire family.

I try to stop thinking on these images. But the picture that keeps replaying in my head over and over is the ending of that Vietnam movie, *Apocalypse Now*, when Marlon Brando is bloody and dying and lying on the floor in the dark, whispering:

"The horror. The horror."

Then the damage control and blame game began.

The shifting positions:

It's the state's fault! It wouldn't let the company drain the black water for fear of killing the trout stocked in the creek.

It's the federal government's fault!

The governor said it's the media's fault!

And the mining company said it was nature's fault. It was "an act of God!"

AN ACT OF GOD.

All I'm thinking is that this is sounding like awfully familiar territory. There was the typical outcry and then a demand for accountability so this could never happen again. Except of course it did in 2000, when an energy company in Kentucky saw its slurry pond collapse and release 300 million gallons of water and 155,000 cubic yards of coal waste. In typical fashion, the federal government jumped into high gear and announced a sweeping review of all 653 coal waste impoundment dams.

Then in January 2006, the world breathlessly watched daily TV reports about thirteen trapped miners stranded underground in West Virginia's Sago Mine. Amazingly, one miner survived this mess. The mine had 208 "serious and substantial" inspection violations the prior year, and I just can't comprehend this cycle of disaster and response. Tragedy and action. Blame and denial. Posturing and lawsuits. Settlements and healing.

But those stories are not even what got me going today. In the middle of my little web searches about Buffalo Creek, I came across a story from July 2005 about West Virginia's Marsh Fork Elementary School, which is situated 400 yards below a 2.8 billion gallon coal waste dam. 400 yards? 2.8 billion gallons! With the kids breathing coal dust and chemicals from the coal silo which sits 150 feet away. Even worse, one of the people who built the dam claims that it was built improperly. And this mining company is another subsidiary of the company responsible for the 2000 disaster in Kentucky.

The only reason this is making any news is that the grandfather of one of the elementary school kids sat on the West Virginia Capitol steps and refused to leave until the governor addressed these rather serious concerns. The guy was just a little curious why the Department of Environmental Protection approved a permit for an additional coal silo adjacent to the school. He was just wondering why in a school of 200 students, three kids and four teachers had died of cancer. And with 240 significant safety violations since 1991, why nothing was being done, like building another school. Away from the madness.

2.8 billion gallons. 2.8 billllllllion. School's not out. School's gone! Oh yeah, and so are the teachers and students and the class pets. Now maybe you're thinking that no one would let this happen to school children. But it already has. In 1966, when 116 kiddies were washed away in Wales in similar fashion. As Moses (well, Charlton Heston) predicted in *Armageddon*: "It happened before. It <u>will</u> happen again."

And it turned out that grandpa wasn't getting anywhere with the state. It bothered me that I had never heard about his story in July 2005, and instead remembered the Famous Hot Dog Eating Contest held that same month when the defending champion competitive eater, Takeru "Tsunami" Kobayashi, won again by eating 49 hot dogs in twelve minutes.

Tsunami, the Competitive Eater?

The arc of the moral universe is long. There's no place like home.

→

- Lesson 37 -

Intelligence is wrapped in many packages

As I sat in class during the first year of law school, I was thoroughly confused when others raised their hands and offered wild legal theories. What I discovered after the fact is that classroom discussion leaders do not always perform as well on exams as the shy, silent student who doesn't utter a peep all semester. Regardless, I don't equate good grades with intelligence.

One psychologist, Robert Sternberg, identifies three types of intelligence in his Triarchic Model:

- Componential Intelligence – analytic, academic abilities to solve problems

- Experiential Intelligence – creativity and insight, the ability to invent, discover, and theorize

- Practical Intelligence – street smarts, ability to adapt to the environment.

I once wrote a letter of recommendation for a student who received a "C" in my class because after many discussions outside of class, I could tell that he had the practical intelligence to succeed in his chosen profession.

Another psychologist, Howard Gardner, suggests that we have Seven Multiple Intelligences: *Linguistic, Logical-Mathematical, Musical, Spatial, Bodily-Kinesthetic, Interpersonal, and Intrapersonal.* As I check off these items, it occurs to me that I am in trouble on Gardner's scale.

- Lesson 38 -

A gentle word of encouragement can last a lifetime

Several weeks into my freshman year in college, I was averaging a "C" in Chemistry with Midterm exams around the corner. I remember calling home, questioning whether I could make it through the semester. My mom just said to buckle down, be determined, and have confidence. For some reason, that got me going, and I made it through the semester.

Sometimes, words of encouragement can spark a fire. Sometimes, they can mean everything.

- Lesson 39 -

Know the consequences of regret

I started out as a Chemistry major in college. When I got bored very quickly with the subject, I realized that I was unknowingly majoring in Friedman. Arnold Friedman.

Mr. Friedman was that favorite high school teacher whom we all were lucky enough to have. Someone who understood how to teach and got thorough enjoyment out of the process. He was wacky, funny, and knowledgeable. He taught Organic Chemistry and Advanced Placement Nuclear Chemistry, which got me two college credits. Mr. Friedman once took us on a field trip to the Brookhaven National Laboratory so we could see a nuclear reactor for ourselves.

When he retired after a twenty year career, several teachers and students threw a retirement party for him, with students expressing how he guided them in the right direction in life. One even expressed how Mr. Friedman saved his life.

I saw Mr. Friedman on TV when I was at my parents' home for Thanksgiving one year. He was on the news, being escorted by the police in handcuffs from his home. Mr. Friedman had opened up a computer school in his basement and was accused of molesting several young children. The understandably frenzied parents were whipped up in a panic, and sought justice.

Mr. Friedman pled guilty to several charges. The police found some disgusting underage magazines and pictures that Mr. Friedman had ordered through the mail. But no physical evidence was found linking him to the charges he faced.

As the years went by, my thoughts about Mr. Friedman ranged between "How on earth could you do this?" to "As sick a person as you are, you were still a great teacher." These emotions were in constant conflict. I found out that he was imprisoned at the Federal Correctional Institution in Oxford, Wisconsin. Several times, I tried to write him a letter, but could not figure out what to say. After a while, I just tried to put this terrible person out of my mind.

Mr. Friedman died alone in his prison cell, divorced by his wife, ridiculed by the public, and shunned in the teaching profession.

A few times each year, I did a web search on his name, to see if anything about the case was discussed. In 2004, I was stunned to find out that a film was made about the incident. *Capturing the Friedmans* was nominated for an Academy Award for Best Documentary and raised several questions and serious doubts about whether any of the abuse alleged actually took place.

I saw the movie when it first came out. And then felt guilty that I never wrote the letter.

- Lesson 40 -

It's good to be the judge! (Part II)

For the few years that I practiced law, I worked on cases with stakes in excess of several millions of dollars. These cases are the polar opposite of the kinds of matters that affect everyday people: landlord-tenant disputes, harassing tactics employed by a collection agency, the auto mechanic who takes cash but never fixes the car. These "street law" cases are ripe for small claims court, but too small for most lawyers to take on. However, most attorneys at some point take on cases for free for those who cannot afford counsel. In fact, state bar associations view "pro bono" work as a moral obligation of every lawyer to serve the public.

I took on pro bono cases for a special family. "John and Iris Smith" were married for a lifetime when John's Social Security disability benefits were terminated wrongfully. Subsequently, he applied for Supplemental Security Income. (SSI) His medical bills were mounting, and the Smiths were running out of money. They lived under the same roof with their three daughters, two sons-in-law, and three grandchildren. John was sent to countless government agencies before seeing me on this matter. Eventually, I got his benefits reinstated. He died that same year.

At the same time, Iris, 58, had developed painful arthritis, colitis, and a rectal lesion which inhibited her ability to work as a seamstress. She was advised by a doctor that she had a tumor that had to be biopsied and removed. However, she was repeatedly denied SSI and disability insurance benefits by the government. Finally, I was granted an administrative hearing in October, where I was able to introduce medical evidence of Iris's condition. In the judge's finding of facts three months later, he stated:

The medical evidence establishes that the claimant has degenerative joint disease of the left hand and right knee, chronic (inactive) ulcerative colitis and a rectal lesion with <u>suspected development of cancer.</u> ...The claimant's past relevant work as a sewing machine operator did not require the performance of work-related activities precluded by the above limitations.

She can still work, judge? Really? Hey, the last time I checked, a seamstress:

1. has to sit to sew (see rectal lesion and ulcerative colitis, which is an inflammatory bowel disease)

2. needs hands to sew (see arthritis)

3. needs a leg to work the foot pedal of a sewing machine (see arthritis)

And I believe that the recent death of Iris's husband and her "suspected development of cancer" might be weighing on her mind. Just maybe.

It's good to be the judge?

Your Mother, Your Honor!

The judge's decision was rendered on December 30 and received by us on January 5. Happy New Year to you too, Your Honor.

Things got worse. On December 16, Iris was rushed to the emergency room complaining of abdominal pain. She had lost 25 pounds in the last three months, and hadn't had a bowel movement for days. It turned out that her obstruction was created by the large tumor mass that was adhering to the wall of the rectal area. The family could not bear to have the doctor inform Iris of the terminal type of cancer that she had.

An attorney's job is to be dispassionate and detached from the emotional aspects of a case. But how could I be? I was upset with the judge's bad ruling and was despondent that this family's matriarch was going to die one day soon. I felt like personally serving His Honor's New Year's Eve dinner: *A yellow lobular adipose tissue consistent with omentum, with metastatic undifferentiated adenocarcinoma.*

In January, I overnighted an emergency motion for re-hearing to the government's Office of Hearings and Appeals. It reads as follows:

IN THE CASE OF:
IRIS SMITH, JOHN SMITH /

MOTION FOR RE-HEARING

COMES NOW, IRIS SMITH, by and through her undersigned counsel, and hereby moves this Court for a re-hearing of the Decision rendered on December 30, from the hearing argued on October 8, and as grounds therefore states the following:

1. The Claimant, IRIS SMITH (MS. SMITH), applied to this Court for disability insurance benefits and for widow's insurance benefits pursuant to the applicable provisions of the Social Security Act.

2. In the Decision rendered on December 30 ("Decision"), and received by the undersigned on January 5, this Court denied the above-referenced benefit requests.

3. Subsequent to the hearing of this cause, MS. SMITH had been hospitalized for the removal of her tumor referenced in the Decision. Upon review of the affected area of the cancerous region, the doctor concluded that said tumor is inoperable and that MS. SMITH only has several months to live.

4. The Decision defines "disability" as "the inability to engage in any substantial gainful activity due to physical or mental impairment(s) which can be expected to either result in death or last for a continuous period of not less than 12 months." (emphasis added)

5. Pursuant to page 6 of the Decision, the Court found that the doctor

"reportedly advised claimant on October 5 that her tumor 'must be removed' (Exhibit 37). However, the record does not contain any medical report of such a procedure being performed."

6. Since an attempt to remove MS. SMITH's inoperable tumor was attempted subsequent to the October 8 hearing in this cause, MS. SMITH is now entitled to disability and widow's benefits since she is now within the definition of "disability" under the Social Security Act and for other reasons under the Act.

[Author's Note: She was eligible back in October too, you nitwits!]

WHEREFORE, Claimant, IRIS SMITH, hereby requests on an <u>expedited and emergency basis</u>, a re-hearing of the Decision rendered on December 30, and any further relief this Court deems equitable and just.

It took the appeals court six months to rule on my emergency motion.

We won.

Iris died that month.

I couldn't work for days.

The practice of law as a litigator has extreme highs and lows. It's hard to describe the intense high of winning a hearing you're supposed to lose, but the rock bottom nature of the lows is tough to take. This was one of those times.

Iris's file was transferred to a new government agency since she passed away. That file was then lost. Her dependents were counting on her Social Security benefits of $10,000. After encountering red tape and making countless long distance telephone calls to Arlington, Virginia; Birmingham, Alabama;

and Baltimore, Maryland, it took several months to receive $7,500. Even though I told the agency upfront that I waived my entitlement to a 25% fee, that $2,500 wasn't included with the $7,500. It took several more months for the Smiths to receive that check.

I've never told the Smiths' story in class, but it serves as a lesson for how I want my students to stand up for what is right and just. Hopefully, they won't all be sitting in jail on contempt charges for uttering: "Your Mother, Your Honor!"

Always be mindful: It's good to be the judge!

- Lesson 41 -

By failing to prepare, you are preparing to fail. When you're finished changing, you're finished.

~ Benjamin Franklin

I am a firm believer in the need to adapt, in that nothing is certain in one's life. And the ticket to this ability to change is one's education. Whether it's pursuing a degree or needing to retrain later in life, education at any level is the core element to sustaining lifelong opportunities in a fluid society. Education leads to self sufficiency and reliance from within, rather than on external sources which may be gone tomorrow.

I thought about that today as I passed the General Motors plant on my way to class. Just a few weeks ago, its workforce was downsized to one shift as GM began the facility's phase out. They are down to 1,000 workers from a high of 2,900. One of my current students is in the lucky grand. And tomorrow, the Ford assembly plant just south of Atlanta will be idled. Opened in 1947 and now lights out. That plant employed as many as 2,000 workers in recent times.

That's it. Education and preparation. On a professional level to give yourself job options. Education and preparation so that you don't get ripped off by a car dealer. Education and preparation when facing a nasty judge. Yes, I get it that you can't stop the forces of nature or the freaks of nature living amongst us. There's nothing that Buffalo Creek Rowland or Judge Rowland could have done differently. But sometimes a little bit of knowledge can help us control or contain some situations.

When a tsunami hit Thailand and surrounding nations in 2004, I had never even heard of the term "tsunami," let alone know that if there's a massive earthquake and you're near the water, that an even more massive wave would be right behind it. I'd like to think I'd run, but easily could've uttered: "Whoa, that just rocked my world. Tsunami? Isn't that the competitive eater dude who scarfed down 49 hot dogs? Pass the mustard and the sun block 15."

But a ten year old British girl named Tilly knew because she learned about tsunamis in her geography class, and because she warned her mom and the hotel people in Phuket, about 100 people were hurried off to safety. Give that girl an "A" and that teacher a big hug. Former President Bill Clinton, the U.N. envoy for the tsunami recovery remarked: "Tilly's story is a simple reminder that education can make a difference between life and death." Me, I might've been dead if put in the exact same circumstance if that little girl weren't around. Wearing the t-shirt I bought at a Thai restaurant in L.A. named Phuket.

Life and death. That brings me back to the grandfather in West Virginia whose grandkid's elementary school sits downstream from 2.8 billion gallons of water mixed with toxic coal sludge. Turns out, after getting blown off by his state officials, he took matters even further into his hands. To gain visibility for his cause, he went on a 455-mile hike to Washington, D.C. and got a meeting with his United States Senator. And that second coal silo building permit which was initially granted was subsequently rejected on the grounds that it would be too close to a school. Ya think?

I smile because I'm not sure how far grandpa will get in raising money to move the school, but I do know he's learned an important lesson. When you are outmatched by the war chest or political clout of opponents, you need to be patient and search for their weak spot to find leverage. And in this case, grandpa's leverage is in the form of embarrassment through media attention. How else could he have gotten an audience with a busy senator? Preparation and a willingness to be persistent.

I attribute our general lack of initiative and drive to our collective fear of change. Fear limits us in profound personal and professional ways, in that it doesn't lead to crushed dreams; rather, fear doesn't even permit dreams to originate, breathe, and germinate. And in all of these years, the only genuine answer that I can muster to combat that fear is education and preparation.

I want so badly to believe in fate and in things happening for a reason, but the educator in me takes over, making me believe that we make our own destiny and control our own fate. I just think that Ben Franklin got it so right in his quotes. But great words are far greater than the person who utters them, and the real hard work is putting those words into action.

By doing. Something.

- Lesson 42 -

Learn at your own pace. You'll get there eventually.

My "welcome to college" moment occurred when I got a C-minus on my very first English paper. It probably didn't help matters that the prior week, I launched a mini toy helicopter which circled the classroom and soft crashed on the professor's head.

As far back as I can remember, I was a slow learner when reaching new levels – junior high, high school, college, and law school. Once I got the hang of it, I started to excel.

As a teacher, I recognize that people don't get things right away, and that every class is an adjustment for students.

- Lesson 43 -

Never crush anyone's dreams

When I was a little kid, I dreamed about playing professional basketball. I played and played for hours. In third grade, we had to write an essay on what we wanted to be when we grew up. I wrote that I wanted to be 6'10" and play in Madison Square Garden. When the teacher handed back my paper, she laughed out loud and said "You can't do that!"

That was the first time someone had crushed my professional dream. Why would a teacher be so unthinking? She may have been right about the 6'10" part, but this molder of young minds lacked the understanding of what negative reinforcement can do to little kids. She also lacked the understanding that height isn't everything for a basketball player.

Teachers, especially in the impressionable K-12 years, are my personal heroes. But they need to be dream builders, not dream destroyers. It's healthy to discuss rational backup career plans, but why spoil youthful exuberance which could flower into the unexpected?

- Lesson 44 -

Find your Light Bulb Moment

As an entering college freshman, I was directionless. During my second semester, I had a memorable English class and for reasons unclear to me, my learning cloud just seemed to lift. Things "clicked" because the professor's keen interest in the subject was infectious and motivated me.

Over the years, I've spent a lot of time thinking on how best to connect with people to get them excited and engaged, whether in a classroom, boardroom, or bored room. I believe that if you show learners that you have a sincere stake in their futures, you have the ability to inspire them on a daily basis, and spark a "light bulb moment."

For every presentation, I try to live up to my own expectations through an acronym:

Perry's L.I.G.H.T. B.U.L.B. Moment for Teachers, Trainers, and Mentors

L. isten to all learners

I. nspire them with real world discussions

G. ive hope to everyone

H. eap compliments on people for quality work

T. each to your strengths

B. e available at all times

U. nderstand that people may lack your life experience or knowledge

L. earn from your learners

B. e willing to walk in anyone's shoes

Have you found your light bulb moment?

FINAL EXAM:
A rubber room, you, a scream

To summarize *Unlocking Your Rubber Room*:
a. It's good to be the judge!
b. Lay low, very low, in the weeds
c. In deal making, make the other side feel like a hero
d. Know the consequences of no regrets
e. Do what you love but don't jeopardize the people you love. Including yourself.
f. Why not us?
g. Intelligence is wrapped in many packages
h. Learn at your own pace. You'll get there eventually.
i. Find your Light Bulb Moment
j. Laugh
k. Think
l. Act
m. All of the above

Now go unlock your rubber room and yell something meaningless out the door. Court and class are dismissed.

III. Graduation

Embracing Your Rubber Room

When I participate in graduation ceremonies, I often imagine delivering my own speech to the graduates, as if I were the commencement speaker:

Good morning Chancellor, President, Deans, Faculty Members, Staff, Students, Friends, and Family Members. Welcome.

Tomorrow is Mother's Day, and before we can shower accolades on the superstars before me, I'd love to recognize the super heroes that got them here. So if you're a mom of a graduate, please stand up for some applause. Keep standing! If you are a grandmother of a graduate, please stand up as well for applause. Keeeeeeeep standing grandma! If you are a graduate, and YOU are a mom as well, please rise for applause. Ladies and gentlemen, please join me in recognizing these miracle workers, for without their encouragement and sacrifice, we would not be here today honoring the bright future of our graduates.

Now moving away from the podium, standing at the edge of the stage and speaking to the grads:

- Every one of you is special.

- Every one of you is a productive member of society.

- Every one of you is what inspires ME - because…

- Every one of you has a story to tell.

I just wish I had the time to hear every one of them, and to be there as your career paths unfold.

You have already accomplished a huge milestone on that journey. The biggest step though was just showing up. That's it. The secret most people don't get until it's too late. Just showing up as young freshmen was a threshold event. Trying something which may be hard for the first time. Experiencing new things, even if it's unknown whether the objective is attainable.

To me, the greatest barriers to success, however you define that, are a fear of the unknown, a fear of change, and a fear of failure. But you need a game plan, and hopefully you can lean a little on what you learned in school to figure out that route. No matter what you do in life, you always will have your education.

I hope you made some lifelong friends here. Frankly, I learned more about life from my peers than from my professors. And I hope you got more than knowledge from your profs because you can get that from a book. I'm hoping you gained insight on whatever subject, and then stamped your own original perspective on how to resolve issues and solve problems.

Many times the things you do won't work. And you will fail at some things you try. That's just a fact of life.

Abraham Lincoln once said: "My great concern is not whether you have failed, but whether you are content with your failure."

And you will make mistakes. A lot of them! Both in your careers and your lives. That's just another fact of life.

But that's okay. The trick is figuring out how to deal with setbacks. Your family and friends will always be there for you. And your education will continually serve as a foundation to get you back on track.

Raise your hand if you've done dumb things in life.

Come on; raise your hands!

Your mama already knows anyway!

Good.

I see a lot of hands up.

Hey, I've made some big mistakes too.

Actually, I feel very lucky to be here today.

Physically, I mean.

You see, at an early age, I was left for dead in a ravine off some highway in upstate New York. Let me read you my obituary:

Perry Binder of Queens, New York, was found dead off Interstate 90 near Buffalo. A trucker discovered his body, dripping with blood and draped with a state trooper's ticket for reckless driving. The apparent cause of death was stupidity. Perry just completed his first year of law school, after graduating with a B.A. in Political Science. He enjoyed watching baseball games with his grandfather, and dreamed of becoming a sports lawyer. He is survived by his mother, father, brother, grandfather, a basketball, no wife, and no kids. Perry was 21 years of age.

Now, as a college educated group, I'm guessing you figured out that this obit was a bit premature? But that's what should have happened to me after pulling a 16-hour graveyard shift loading and unloading passenger baggage in a downtown bus depot, then jumping in my car and driving the second leg of my 140 mile roundtrip commute.

At highway speed and just five minutes from home, I fell asleep at the wheel.

I blasted the car stereo, rolled down the windows, and sucked down a gallon of coffee. The warning signs were all there, but I just kept going and going.

Eventually, my eyes closed as my hands slipped off the steering wheel. The car veered to the right, right off the road, smashing into the side of a parked flatbed. That truck miraculously prevented the car from flying into a grassy ravine. It was off on the road's shoulder, so the trucker could catch up on some sleep. Luckily, he was okay, but I think I woke him up at the same moment I opened my eyes.

In shock, losing blood and coherent thought, I wandered aimlessly down into the ravine. I wanted more than anything to lie down in a fetal position, close my eyes and pray for some help. But I knew that I needed to stay conscious.

In the days before cell phones, it was fortunate that the trucker had a CB radio. He called for paramedics who arrived quickly and gave me fluids and oxygen. I was weak but remained in this world, as the ambulance raced to the hospital.

Two broken hands and an extremely smashed head. I had a seat belt on, but no air bag to cushion the blow.

To this day, I wonder what forces put a flatbed truck in my path. During recovery, I thought a lot about my brush with certain death. All I knew was that I was alive and awakened to the fragility of life.

Invited guests - usually my class is a little more upbeat and a lot less harrowing than this anecdote! But I relay this experience today to my students for many reasons.

- It's a story of turning a negative into a positive. This near fatal mistake made me appreciate life just a little more. To be curious and try things, regardless of what others think. I encourage you graduates to be adventurous!

- The experience taught me about limits. That hand-in-hand with taking risks, I better assess the dangers and consequences associated with the risks.

- It allowed me to write another chapter in my personal and professional life. It clarified and focused my attention on going after things that made me happy.

- It allowed me time to meet my wife, witness the birth of a child, and then another.

- I don't know if it's a coincidence that my day-in and day-out work is with students whose age mirror my own at the time of the car accident. I do know that I stand here today proud of what you've achieved in my class and at this university. I am excited about your very bright futures!

- I wanted to tell you something about me that you didn't get in class, because no matter how well you think you know people, they have stories within them that can surprise you.

To quote Franklin D. Roosevelt, "We are not prisoners of fate, but only prisoners of our own minds." Graduates, each of you must unlock your mind – your rubber room – and blaze a path built on reason and purpose. Life is too short to spend it bouncing around like a random and aimless ball in a game of Pong.® And whether you are 20, 30, 40, 50, 60, 70, or 80 years young, it is never too late to test the boundaries of your dreams.

Finally, I want all of you gathered in front of me to please lose the title of "former" student, because you will be my students for many years to come. And I expect in return that I can become your student, as I learn about your professional successes, trials, and tribulations.

- Every one of you is special.

- Every one of you is a productive member of society.

- Every one of you is what inspires me – because...

- Every one of you has a story to tell.

What will your next journey be?

Epilogue

Rub·ber Room *(noun)*
An isolated place where schools send unruly
teachers awaiting disciplinary proceedings

There is a symmetry to every college semester, with a set number of weeks and exams at fixed intervals. Just like a Hollywood screenplay has three acts, I love the predictability that the semester structure brings. After teaching for a while, I became adept at seeing common class trends and defining plot points along an arc - when to expect enthusiastic student participation, when students might be stressed or losing confidence, when to pull back on the material or forge full speed ahead. While the structure is predictable, every semester has an energy and a life of its own.

Someone once asked me how I can teach the same subjects year after year without getting bored. My answer back: "Do you think that a recording artist gets bored singing the same song for the past thirty years?" It may be the same song, but there's a different interpretation and a fluid audience each time. A performer can kill one night, and then fall flat the next evening if the crowd's chemistry isn't there. The song remains the same, but those sitting in on the sessions may not always be on the same page. Yes, the course material is similar from year to year, but meeting different students each time is the secret part of the equation which keeps things lively, unpredictable, and exciting.

A teacher's job is to keep things fresh and provocative, regardless of mood, subject, or student engagement. The show must always go on. The good news is that there's ample opportunity to shift gears from week to week to capture attention and to captivate.

A lot has happened in my career since that day I ascended the escalator heading to my first law job and declared: "This is gonna suck!" Of course it doesn't really suck, if you're the right person for the job. The life of a litigator is a rewarding job for many.

Naturally, my curious students ask me why I don't practice law anymore. The best answer I can come up with is an analogy from the movie, *Good Will Hunting*, when psychologist Robin Williams is discussing personal relationships with patient, Matt Damon. Damon just had a perfect first date with Minnie Driver, and he tells Williams that he's never going to call her again. To which a surprised Williams inquires why. Damon explains that the date was so perfect, that he didn't want to ruin that memory or image, and risk an imperfect second date. The psychologist smiles and reminds his young patient that he's not so perfect himself, and neither is his recent date. The trick he says is to take a risk and discover whether you're perfect for each other.

Being a teacher is not a perfect profession, and I know I'm an imperfect teacher. But we're perfect for each other. I've learned, changed, grown, and gotten back more than I bargained for in many courtrooms and classrooms.

Today, I am refreshed and ready, but already messed up on the first day of the current term in front of 120 students. While I remembered to bring the syllabus, I forgot to bring their outline for the first unit. The class was already confused about the first assignment.

Maybe I have an overactive imagination or a hypersensitive ear, but I could've sworn I heard a student mutter under her breath:

"This professor sucks!"

ACKNOWLEDGEMENTS

I once heard Michael Corleone say that he keeps his friends close but his enemies closer. The Godfather apparently never sat down to write a book, because once the second draft is completed, the editing process becomes one of collaboration with close friends, family members, and colleagues. In that vein, I'd like to thank Bridget Binder, Dave Binder, Jill Brubaker, Ellie Diaz, Julia Goodman, Carin Gordon, Blaine Parker, and Vinny Picardi for their collective wisdom and support.

In addition, I want thank my parents, June and Jack Binder, for showing me the importance of education, Barbara Weston for sparking my interest in writing, and novelist Stephen King for bothering to pen *On Writing*. Finally, I want to acknowledge Professor Tom Green for giving me the opportunity to teach my first college class. He may have seen something in me that I didn't see at the time, or was just desperate to fill that class with a prof on the day before the semester began.

ABOUT THE AUTHOR

Perry Binder is an Assistant Professor of Legal Studies at Georgia State University's Robinson College of Business in Atlanta, Georgia. In 2008, Perry received the MBA students' *Crystal Apple Teaching Award,* and in 2005, he received Robinson's *Teaching Excellence Award.*

Perry is an energetic public speaker who enjoys interacting with diverse audiences nationwide. Further information about Perry and *Unlocking Your Rubber Room* may be found at www.YourRubberRoom.com.